Edward Elgar

An illustrated life of Sir Edward Elgar

(1857-1934)

Michael Messenger

A Shire book

Sir Edward Elgar: portrait by Phillip Burne-Jones, purchased by the Worcester Corporation and hanging in the Guildhall, Worcester.

Contents

British Library Cataloguing in Publication Data: Messenger, Michael (Michael Frederick). Edward Elgar: an illustrated life of Sir Edward Elgar, 1857–1934. – (Lifelines; 46) 1. Elgar, Edward, 1857–1934 2. Composers – England – Biography I. Title 780.9'2. ISBN 0 7478 0621 7.

ACKNOWLEDGEMENTS
Except where otherwise stated, all paintings, photographs or objects illustrated are in the ownership of the Elgar Foundation, which is responsible for the Elgar Birthplace Museum, and I am grateful to the Director and staff at the Birthplace for their ready co-operation in providing photographs and other material for this book and to the Elgar Will Trust for permission to quote from Elgar's letters. The cover portrait and the illustration on page 23 are reproduced courtesy of Norman Perryman, who retains the copyright for both paintings. The original photograph of the casket on page 31 is by John Harcup and the colour illustrations on pages 2, 27, 42 (top), 49 and 50 have been specially photographed for this book by Neil Woolford; the exterior views of the area on pages 8, 12, 18 (top), 46 (top), 59 (both) and 60 are by David A. Ross, LRPS.

Cover: *Sir Edward Elgar: detail from 'Enigma', painted by Norman Perryman and displayed at the Elgar Birthplace Museum.*

Published in 2005 by Shire Publications Ltd, Cromwell House, Church Street, Princes Risborough, Buckinghamshire HP27 9AA, UK. Website: www.shirebooks.co.uk Copyright © 2005 by Michael Messenger. First published 2005. Number 46 in the Lifelines series. ISBN 0 7478 0621 7.

Printed in Malta by Gutenberg Press Limited, Gudja Road, Tarxien PLA 19, Malta.

William Henry Elgar, aged about thirty-five.

Background and apprenticeship, 1857–91

On 2nd June 1857, in the Worcestershire village of Broadheath, a son was born to William Henry and Ann Elgar; they named him Edward William, and against all the odds he was to become one of Britain's finest ever composers. It is a remarkable story of how one man, aided by a dedicated wife, overcame the disadvantages of birth, limited education, lack of formal training, religious prejudice and even his own uncertain temperament to become the recipient of many of the highest honours that his country could bestow upon him. No one on that summer's day in rural Worcestershire could have foreseen what lay ahead.

At that time, William Henry Elgar was a piano tuner who had moved to Worcester in 1841, and it was there that he met and in 1848 married Ann Greening. The daughter of a farm-worker, Ann was – perhaps remarkably given the social attitudes and distinctions of the time interested in the arts and with a great appetite for reading. Her daughter Lucy later described her as 'romantic by temperament and poetic by nature', adding:

> She had the unmistakable air of good breeding, which like the perfect manners of the true gentlewoman is felt without being defined – being highly educated with fine literary tastes, and a deep reader all her life.

Ann often drove out with her husband when he was on business and while he was tuning pianos she would sketch the churches and the local scenery. In 1852 she converted to Catholicism, possibly introduced to it through her husband's connection with St George's Roman Catholic Church in Worcester, where, despite being a confirmed Protestant, he had been appointed organist in 1846.

The cottage at Broadheath where Elgar was born, from the watercolour by J. C. Buckler, 1857; the painting actually shows members of the Elgar family, with Mr and Mrs Elgar and their daughter Lucy in the foreground.

Ann Elgar holding the young Edward.

It was a modest enough background, and the humble cottage in Broadheath where Edward was born was a reflection of that. The family had moved out of the city to Broadheath in 1856, by which time William was already well established within the musical life of the city, and it is not surprising that the children should in their turn become involved. Indeed, they seem to have been a gifted family, with Edward's elder sister Lucy producing some delightful flower studies in watercolour and his younger brother Frank playing the oboe, while the death of young Jo at the early age of seven may have been more than just a domestic tragedy since the Elgars already regarded him as 'the Beethoven of the family'.

Edward was the couple's fourth child and their second son. Although he was only two years old when the family moved back into the city, he seems to have developed a lifelong attachment to the area and to the modest cottage in which he had been born, returning to the locality regularly and, many years later, bringing his wife and friends to see the cottage. As a boy, he helped his father and his uncle Henry in their music shop, which

Edward aged eight with his younger brother Jo, who died at the age of seven some two years after this photograph was taken.

6

The Elgar Brothers' music shop on the High Street, Worcester; it has since been demolished but the site is marked by a plaque.

had by now become firmly established in the High Street in Worcester, selling pianos and sheet music. Edward was educated at two Catholic schools, but it was probably his mother's influence that led to his lifelong enthusiasm for books and reading on a wide variety of topics. When he left school at fifteen he was desperately anxious to take up music as a career, but the resources of a local music retailer and piano tuner made this impossible and young Edward was sent to work in the office of a local solicitor; clearly he found this an uncongenial profession since he left a year later to help his father with the family business. This provided plentiful opportunities for him to become acquainted with music at first hand, but it would have counted for little had it not been for his temperament, described by his mother as

Nervous, sensitive and kind
Displays no vulgar frame of mind.

It seems clear that he had inherited his mother's responsiveness to the arts – and to the countryside generally, which was to serve as an inspiration to him throughout his life.

Sensitive he may have been, but he was also a very determined young man, and that he used his time in the music shop to good effect is clear from his comment in 1904 that 'I saw and learnt a great deal

7

Worcester Cathedral, where the music had a formative influence on the young Edward Elgar.

about music from the stream of music that passed through my father's establishment'. He went on to say:

> When I resolved to become a musician and found that the exigencies of life would prevent me from getting any tuition, the only thing to do was to teach myself. I read everything, played everything, and heard everything that I possibly could ... I am self-taught in the matter of harmony, counterpoint, form, and, in short, the whole 'mystery' of music ...

He absorbed music like blotting paper and listened to whatever he could, whether it be recitals by visiting celebrities, concerts by local amateur societies or the choral services in the nearby Anglican cathedral. From his father came also the opportunity to become involved in local music-making, and he was introduced to the Worcester Glee Club, the core of which was provided by choristers from Worcester Cathedral. There he played the violin and acted as accompanist for two or three years, apparently performing with precocious talent, and the local glee

Studio portrait of Edward while still in his teens.

clubs (there were two for some years) also provided opportunities for the young man to try out some of his early compositions and arrangements.

Opportunities for composition and playing were not limited to the weekly Glee Club meetings, however, and, besides occasionally substituting for his father at the organ during the services at St George's Church, his services as a violinist were increasingly in demand by local orchestras and choral societies. He even replaced his father as orchestra leader in some cases and occasionally performed as a soloist. In 1877 he was appointed leader of the newly formed Worcester Amateur Instrumental Society, and he made a few weekly trips to London, where he had violin lessons from Adolphe Pollitzer. He concluded that he was unlikely to succeed in a career as a performer, although he did continue to play locally, appearing in his first Worcester Three Choirs Festival in 1878.

In the meantime he had taught himself to play the bassoon and with his brother Frank, his friend

The Powick Quintet, 1875: Frank Exton (flute), Hubert Leicester (flute), Frank Elgar (oboe) and William Leicester (clarinet) with Edward Elgar (bassoon) standing in the centre.

Hubert Leicester and two other friends formed a wind quintet, for which he wrote some pieces of music. He also joined the band at the County Lunatic Asylum at Powick, between Worcester and Malvern; this comprised an unlikely group of a piano with string and wind instruments (including a euphonium), but the practicalities of writing and arranging music for such an ensemble must have stood him in good stead during his subsequent career. In short, the young Elgar was anxious to seize whatever opportunities presented themselves in order to develop his musical skills, and even to create them where none already existed.

He was soon to add a new string to his bow: conducting. In August 1882 he appears to have replaced the scheduled conductor for a programme of music given by the Worcester Instrumental Society for the British Medical Association – an event that had an added significance for Elgar as it was there that he met and struck up a close friendship with Charles Buck, a Yorkshire doctor, which was to endure throughout his life. During these formative years, from Edward's teens until his marriage in 1889, the life he enjoyed (or possibly endured) was very much that of the locally based journeyman musician, playing and giving lessons, and the same may be said of most of his compositions during this period.

Elgar's desire to compose was manifested while he was still a boy, when he began to write the music for a children's play, but it was not until nearly forty years later that any of that music reached fruition, when the mature Elgar reworked some of the themes as *The Wand of Youth* suite. In 1872 he wrote a birthday song, *The Language of Flowers*, for his sister Lucy, but it was not long before these essentially domestic pieces were supplemented by arrangements and original compositions designed for wider audiences. Many of them were tailored to specific groups, including the 'Introductory Overture' he composed for the 1st Worcestershire Artillery Volunteers' Amateur Christy Minstrels, the pieces he wrote first for the Worcester glee clubs and the *Harmony Music* (sometimes described as 'Shed Music') that he composed for his wind quintet.

The *Harmony Music* of 1878 provides a link with Elgar's private life, too. By this time Elgar had grown to manhood, and photographs of him during these years, though highly stylised, show a handsome young man, already sporting the then fashionable moustache and suggesting more than a hint of introspection. Despite this, he seems to have retained a keen sense of humour – even if it did incline towards schoolboy japes – and he certainly had the ability to make and keep friends. He entitled the second of the four pieces of the *Harmony Music* 'Nelly Shed', otherwise Helen Jessie Weaver, and no fewer than three of the polkas he wrote for the Powick band between 1881 and 1883 are also associated with her name.

Helen was a Worcester girl, the daughter of a shoe-shop proprietor in the High Street, and it is probable that she and Edward had known one another since childhood. She was some three years younger than

Edward Elgar at the age of twenty-three.

him, and musical, pursuing her violin studies at the Leipzig Conservatoire. In January 1883 Edward visited that city, where he heard music by Schumann and Wagner – though it is difficult not to believe that the presence of Helen in Leipzig was the main reason for the visit since there is no doubt that he had become very attached to her. It is probable that the pair came to an understanding there, and after she returned home in the summer they announced their engagement. The engagement lasted less than a year, however, possibly because of religious difficulties (Helen was a Nonconformist and Edward a Roman

Catholic), possibly because of Helen's indifferent health since she had developed tuberculosis.

Edward was devastated by her decision to break off their engagement and, ever prone as he was to violent mood swings, was plunged into despair. He took a brief holiday in Scotland, a memento of which survives in his violin piece *Une Idylle*, dedicated to 'Miss E.E. of Inverness' (a fleeting antidote to the disappointment of his broken engagement perhaps), and the first of his compositions to appear in print. In 1885 Helen Weaver left for New Zealand, where her health did improve, but the link between the two was broken – although there is some evidence that Elgar did not entirely forget his first love and that it was Helen and not Lady Mary Lygon whom the composer portrayed some years later as the thirteenth subject in his celebrated *Enigma Variations*. In the meantime Elgar had continued to play and to compose, writing some liturgical pieces for St George's Church, where he succeeded his father as organist in November 1885, and a number of orchestral pieces; one such was the *Sérénade mauresque* of 1883, which was performed by W. C. Stockley's Orchestra in Birmingham, another *Sevillana*, played at the Crystal Palace in London less than a month after its première in Worcester.

Nevertheless the need to teach remained critical, even though Elgar himself disliked it and appears to have been temperamentally unsuited

to it, describing 'teaching in general … [as] like turning a grindstone with a dislocated shoulder'. Needs must, however, and in 1883 the young man extended his teaching of violin and piano to the Malvern area. In 1886 he began to give lessons to a thirty-seven year old spinster, Caroline Alice Roberts, daughter of the late Major-General Sir Henry Gee Roberts, KCB, of the Indian Army. At the time Alice was looking after her widowed mother, but she herself was an accomplished lady with literary

The organ of St George's Roman Catholic Church in Worcester, where Edward first assisted and then in 1885 succeeded his father as organist.

Alice Roberts, *c*.1885, four years before her marriage to Edward.

pretensions, having had a novel published some four years earlier and writing a substantial amount of poetry. Alice was driven to Malvern for her weekly lesson by the family coachman, who was later reported to have said that he 'thought there was more in it than the music'. There certainly was, for in September 1888 Alice and Edward became engaged; Lady Roberts had died just over fifteen months earlier, but Alice's relatives were for the most part horrified, some going so far as to ostracise her. Not only was Elgar an obscure musician, but he was the son of a shopkeeper and, to compound the situation, a Roman Catholic in a period in which social distinctions were sharply drawn

'When Chivalry lifted up her lance on high': a drawing that decorates the manuscript score of *Froissart*, the first of Elgar's compositions to be performed at the Three Choirs Festival.

and Catholics were treated with suspicion if not outright hostility.

Alice, however, recognised the quality of the man and never wavered in her faith in him, and it is impossible to overestimate the practical and psychological support she offered during the three decades of their marriage. Already in 1888 she had given him a poem that she had written, *Love's Grace*, and this became the immediate inspiration for Edward's romantic composition *Salut d'Amour*, still one of the composer's most popular pieces. Alice responded by continuing to provide him with further poems that she had written, and Elgar set a number of these to music.

Edward and Alice were married at Brompton Oratory in May 1889 and immediately made plans to move to London, probably at Alice's instigation, where Edward would be in a position to advance his career more effectively. The first few months of marriage seem to have been idyllic, and the daily diary kept by Alice, even when it deals with mundane matters, suggests a remarkable sense of intimacy through its frequent use of the personal language, often reminiscent of baby-talk, developed by the two and maintained throughout the whole of their life together. It is clear that the couple's happiness temporarily dispelled the continuing sense of inferiority and resentment still felt by Elgar, now in his thirties, which stemmed from the slights and rebuffs he had received as a young man. This lack of confidence probably accounts for the pleasure he took in public recognition and awards, and may have contributed to the fits of depression to which he was subject and even to his tendency towards hypochondria. Much of this was banished during the early months of marriage, and there is little doubt that the liaison with Alice, coupled with the optimism for the future that she held, did give him greater confidence.

There was good news on the musical front, too, with the decision by the Worcester Three Choirs Festival committee to commission a new work by Elgar. The result was the overture *Froissart*, which received

'Forli', the house at Malvern Link where the Elgars lived from 1891 to 1899.

its première in Worcester Cathedral on 9th September 1890, less than a month after the Elgars' daughter was born; they named the child Carice Irene, and she was to be their only child. Edward's initial reaction to fatherhood seems to have been entirely positive; he described his daughter as 'a pretty little thing' – though he did mention that nursing her was fatal to his trousers and that he would as soon nurse an 'automatic irrigator'!

In London, however, things were not going so well. Although the prestigious music-publishing firm of Novello accepted *Froissart* and Elgar had managed to place a few of his smaller works with publishers, there was no sign of the wider recognition for which the Elgars had hoped. The family needed the regular income that teaching could provide, but the unpalatable truth was that there were better known and better qualified teachers of music working in the metropolis, and neither was Edward's cause helped by the periodic bouts of ill health from which he suffered – real enough no doubt, though probably exacerbated by anxiety and depression. Early in 1891 the couple bowed to the inevitable and abandoned London for Worcestershire, where Elgar resumed his former life of teaching, performing and composing. They settled in Malvern, moving into the house in Malvern Link that they themselves called 'Forli' in June 1891. It was to be their home for almost eight years – eight years that would prove significant in the composer's developing artistic maturity.

Malvern, 1891–1904

Elgar was already working on a cantata, *The Black Knight*, which was performed by the Worcestershire Festival Choral Society, and the same body was responsible for the première three years later of *From the Bavarian Highlands*, inspired by a visit to the area and Alice's translation of local folk-songs. It is a striking example of the extent to which Elgar was inspired by places, and the same is undoubtedly true of the Malvern Hills, amidst which he now lived. In 1898, for example, in response to a commission from the Leeds Festival, he composed *Caractacus*, the tale of a British warrior chief driven westwards by the Romans; the choice was prompted by a suggestion from his mother that he write something about British Camp (the Herefordshire Beacon) near the southern end of the Malverns, and the cantata was completed in the peace of 'Birchwood', a country cottage some 4 miles (6 km) from the centre of Malvern that Elgar had rented. Clearly he found

Alice and Edward in 1897: a studio portrait taken while the couple were on holiday in Garmisch, Germany.

The Malvern Hills, which provided much of the inspiration for some of Elgar's early works.

British Camp, which inspired *Caractacus* and where the profile still reflects the ancient earthworks.

the atmosphere of 'Birchwood' conducive to work since he continued to occupy it even after the family moved in 1899 to a house in Malvern Wells that they called 'Craeg Lea'; the name is typical of Elgar's love of word-play since it comprises an anagram of 'Elgar' and the initial letters of Alice, Carice and Edward himself.

In the meantime he had made contact with August Jaeger, a music reader with the publishing firm Novello, who was to prove not just a firm friend but also a committed supporter of Elgar's music; his influence furthered its publication and his suggestions were welcomed by the composer. Jaeger was to feature as one of Elgar's 'friends pictured within' the *Enigma Variations*, in which he was described as 'Nimrod', another characteristic piece of word-play by Elgar relating the German word *Jaeger* to the mighty hunter of the Bible. Other 'friends' included Dora Penney ('Dorabella'), the Malvern architect 'Troyte' Griffith, Winifred Norbury ('W N '), who helped to proof-read *Caractacus* and subsequently assisted in the creation of the Worcestershire Philharmonic Society, his wife Alice, and even Dan the bulldog, belonging to Hereford organist G. R. Sinclair ('G.R.S.'); the thirteenth variation is designated only '***' and was long thought to represent Lady Mary Lygon, who was on a sea voyage at the time of the *Enigma*'s composition; this belief was encouraged by Alice, but the yearning character of the music suggests that it may actually reflect Elgar's feelings for his first love Helen Weaver.

August Jaeger, the 'Nimrod' of the *Enigma Variations*.

The *Variations* were an immediate success when they were performed in London in 1899 and, more than any other single work, helped to bring Elgar's music to the attention of a wider audience, but the composer still taught locally and remained heavily involved in the local music scene. In 1897, for example, he had founded the Worcestershire Philharmonic Society, with himself as conductor, but in 1902, disgusted by what he saw as the ill-preparedness of the chorus, he stormed out of a rehearsal and resigned his position in favour of his colleague Granville Bantock. That experience coloured his thinking, for when in 1903, with the aid of Troyte Griffith, he launched the Malvern Concert Club he ensured that it only 'bought in' professional recitals and that its own members did not perform for the club.

It is clear that he was not one to tolerate slovenliness – certainly not in the making of music – and his own conducting, though not technically of the first rank, could inspire musicians through his deeply expressive eyes and mobile hands. Even so, he was far from the archetypal portrait of a musician, with his daughter Carice later stating

Elgar's lifelong friend Arthur Troyte Griffith, the Malvern architect and long-serving secretary of the Malvern Concert Club, which Elgar founded in 1903. (From an original sketch by Illingworth Varley)

that he 'looked more like a military officer than an artist', and he was as happy cycling the country lanes around Malvern, discussing literature, flying kites with Troyte from the top of the Malverns, carrying out scientific experiments or attending horse-racing in Worcester as he was playing or composing music. He was acutely sensitive to criticism, and he could be dismissive of his more academically trained contemporaries, especially when he thought that their often inferior music was preferred to his own, but the 'devil on his shoulder', and Alice's encouragement no doubt, meant that the urge to compose remained, with alternating periods of exultation and black despair coupled with bouts of ill health.

Music seemed to be pouring from him now: the violin piece *Chanson de matin* and the song cycle *Sea Pictures* (with one of the songs setting a poem by Alice) followed in 1899, and then Elgar settled to his most ambitious project so far – *The Dream of Gerontius*. A large scale work

Elgar, an enthusiastic cyclist, outside 'Craeg Lea', with his daughter Carice behind the gate.

21

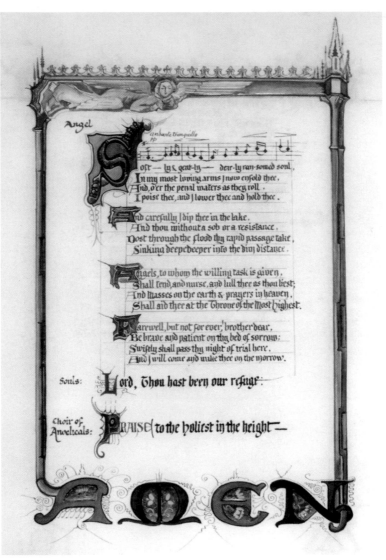

Page from an illuminated copy of Newman's *The Dream of Gerontius*,
formerly owned by Elgar.

for three soloists, chorus and orchestra, it uses the text of the long
religious poem by Cardinal John Henry Newman that concerns the
soul's journey to God after death, and Elgar created from it a powerful
work, one which he himself described as 'the best of me'. It was written
for the Birmingham Festival of 1900, and Elgar and his close friends

'Elgar's Dream': a realisation of Elgar's *The Dream of Gerontius* by the artist Norman Perryman, whose large watercolour (designed as a triptych) is hanging at Symphony Hall in Birmingham.

– not least Jaeger, who had made innumerable suggestions during composition – were optimistic. It was finished at 'Birchwood' in August and performed at the beginning of October, but the performance itself was extremely poor and the resulting fiasco plunged Elgar into a welter of bitterness and despair.

The quality of the work was recognised by more perspicacious musicians and critics, however, not least Hans Richter, who had conducted that first disastrous performance, and it was taken up by Julius Buths, an influential German director, who conducted a triumphant performance in Düsseldorf at the end of 1901. Germany, it seemed, was quicker to recognise musical genius than many of Elgar's own countrymen, and his international status was confirmed. The compliment was returned, for the Elgars clearly enjoyed the country, holidaying there on several occasions, with Edward listening enthusiastically to music by Wagner and the emerging Richard Strauss. The latter, in 1902, was to acclaim 'Meister' Elgar as 'the first English progressivist'.

There were those in Britain who *did* acknowledge his ability, including the critic Ernest Newman, who first met the composer in 1901, Frank Schuster, who was a wealthy and influential patron of the arts, and the composer Charles Villiers Stanford, who persuaded the syndics at Cambridge University to award Elgar an honorary doctorate of music in 1900. This must have afforded Elgar some amusement as well as satisfaction, bearing in mind his thinly veiled hostility towards what he felt was an academically biased musical establishment – though the Elgar finances were still such that he initially hesitated to accept the degree and his academic robes were bought only with the aid of a collection amongst his friends, led by Alfred Rodewald, a wealthy Liverpool industrialist.

It was with Rodewald and Granville Bantock that Elgar founded the humorously titled 'Skip the Pavement Club', an informal gathering of kindred spirits who met, talked, smoked and drank after concerts; it provided just one of the subjects for Elgar's characteristic cartoons, some of which lampooned himself while not even royalty escaped his

Members of the 'Skip the Pavement Club': Alfred Rodewald, Edward Elgar and Granville Bantock at Rodewald's house at Saughall near Chester in 1902.

sense of the absurd, and his letters to friends and his young daughter were frequently embellished with these doodles. The membership of the 'Club' was widened to include a few close friends such as Charles Grindrod, a Malvern water-cure doctor and amateur photographer who took some perceptive studies of Elgar, and Ivor Atkins, the organist of Worcester Cathedral.

Atkins had first been attracted to Elgar's music at the première of *Froissart* and the two became firm friends, while Schuster's

Queen Victoria

Above: 'We are ... amused' – at least, Edward Elgar presumably was when he sketched this caricature of Queen Victoria, possibly for his young daughter Carice.

Ivor Atkins, organist at Worcester Cathedral and another of Elgar's personal friends. (Studio portrait by Elliott and Fry, 1899)

significance extended beyond his support for the music. The latter was part of a German-Jewish banking family and sought the acquaintance of famous musicians; he also enjoyed a wide circle of well-connected friends and in 1902 introduced Elgar to the Stuart Wortleys. Elgar was to find in Alice Stuart Wortley, daughter of the celebrated painter Millais, a further source of musical inspiration, and a friendship between the two families developed, with the composer describing Alice as his 'Windflower'.

Further honours were to follow the Cambridge doctorate, partly in recognition of his growing significance of course, but Elgar himself was not slow to cultivate royalty and those of influence. Queen Victoria, for example, accepted the dedication of *Caractacus* and, following her death in 1901, Elgar set himself to write an Ode for the Coronation of Edward VII in 1902. For its finale Elgar adapted part of the *Pomp and Circumstance March* no. 1 that he had written during the previous year, and which included a tune that the composer himself prophesied would 'knock 'em flat'; the result was *Land of Hope and Glory*, the one tune everyone associates with Elgar, a stalwart of the last night of the Proms, and calculated to link the composer irrevocably with the image of Empire. Elgar was certainly a man of his time, and in 1902 national fervour was running high because of the Boer War, but he was deeply sensitive and mindless jingoism was no part of his character, and the full range of his music reflects this.

For his next major work, for instance, he turned once again to a religious theme, settling upon *The Apostles* as the first part of an ambitious trilogy of oratorios. It was something that had been in his mind for some time and, though the whole project was never to reach completion, *The Apostles* was finished in August 1903, two months before its first performance at the Birmingham Festival, which Elgar himself conducted. This time the performance was worthy of the music and the critics' reaction ranged from guarded approval to downright enthusiasm; public reaction to what was regarded as a less approachable work than *Gerontius* was more muted, but Elgar, who was exhausted after having prepared all the parts himself, was satisfied. He now wanted nothing more than to escape from the rigours of composition and spend some time in the open air.

Within a fortnight, though, he had to preside at the first concert of the Malvern Concert Club, given by the Brodsky Quartet, whom he greatly admired, and then came the devastating news that his great friend Rodewald had died at the age of forty-three. Elgar professed himself heart-broken at the loss of his 'dearest, kindest, best friend',

Alice Stuart Wortley, Elgar's 'Windflower'. (Watercolour by Burne-Jones, after a portrait by Millais)

and it is little wonder that Elgar and his wife felt the need to escape. Towards the end of November they left England for an extended holiday in Italy, and there Edward was able to rest and his health improved – though the urge to compose was never far away and his stay at Alassio inspired the concert overture *In the South*, one of his most popular works.

27

The idyll was broken, however, when Elgar received an invitation to dine with the King, and the Elgars curtailed their holiday to return for the event at Marlborough House on 3rd February 1904. During March Elgar was honoured by a three-day festival of his works at the Royal Opera House, Covent Garden, with royalty present at all three concerts, and a few weeks later came the news that the composer was to receive a knighthood. By then, perhaps in anticipation of the news, the Elgars had arranged to leave the familiar surroundings of Malvern for Hereford.

Hereford, 1904–11

The Elgars moved into 'Plâs Gwyn' in Hereford, an imposing house in which Alice thought that great music could be written, without any apparent regrets at leaving Malvern – though Edward did indicate that he was sorry to be away from his friend Troyte Griffith, even suggesting that Troyte buy a bicycle so that he could ride the 20 miles (32 km) to visit them at their new home. The first year was punctuated by complaints from Elgar about his health, his lack of productiveness, his shortage of money – all recurrent themes – with even his visits to the Continent to oversee performances of *The Apostles* and the receipt of honorary degrees from Leeds and Durham failing to lift his spirits. Oxford University was to follow suit in 1905, and in the same year the City

'Plâs Gwyn', the Elgars' house in Hereford.

Elgar, accompanied by the Mayor, Hubert Leicester, and wearing the academic robes he had received from Yale University, leaving the Guildhall, where he was awarded the Freedom of the City of Worcester in 1905.

W. H. Elgar, Edward's father, watching the procession from the first-floor window of his shop.

The silver casket presented to Sir Edward Elgar at the ceremony.

of Worcester, prompted by Edward's boyhood friend Hubert Leicester, who was the current mayor, honoured its native son by awarding Elgar the honorary Freedom of the City; it is a touching example of filial recognition that as the ceremonial procession wound its way past the Elgar Brothers' music shop on the High Street Edward bared his head to his now infirm father, who was watching from an upstairs window.

In that same year the University of Birmingham offered Elgar the newly endowed Peyton Chair of Music, a position that he accepted with some reluctance. His initial lecture, 'A Future for English Music', proved highly controversial when Elgar, never the most tactful of men, voiced forthright criticism of English music composed during the previous quarter-century, and neither was his second lecture, delivered late in 1905 on 'English Composers', calculated to appease the musical establishment of the time, however much posterity may have endorsed his views. Further lectures continued to provoke controversy, although it was not until 1908 that he finally resigned the Chair.

Neither were the compositions produced during the eighteen months following his move to Hereford an overwhelming success. The *Introduction and Allegro for Strings* was a failure at its first performance at the Queen's Hall in London, and his conducting commitments with the London Symphony Orchestra and in the United States (apparently to raise money) left him little time to compose; the part-song *Evening Scene*, though one of his best, is little more than a miniature and Elgar's ambition was to write 'big' pieces. He did manage a holiday in the Mediterranean, however, and with warmth and rest he found he could turn once again to his biblical trilogy, ideas for which he had been jotting down for some time. The proposal was that the second part, entitled *The Kingdom*, be performed at the Birmingham Triennial Festival of 1906, three years after the première of *The Apostles*, but it was not until the last two months of 1905 that he resumed work on it in earnest.

It coincided with a period of deep depression, possibly stemming in part from the exacting nature of the composition itself, linked perhaps to the success that Elgar had already achieved, and the lionisation and added social commitments that went with it; almost a year earlier his friend Jaeger had expressed concern at the danger of 'success artistic and social' adversely affecting Elgar's 'muse', and the final period of the composer's life, following the death of his wife, confirms that without a powerful spur Elgar was only too ready to abandon the

Alice in the drawing room at 'Plâs Gwyn'.

Gethsemane of composition. For the moment, however, he had Alice at his elbow – encouraging him, nursing him, providing practical support through, for example, the preparation of his manuscript paper, maintaining the house and acting as hostess to visitors.

Paradoxically perhaps, given the theme of *The Kingdom*, its composition coincided with a slackening of the ties that bound him to the Roman Catholic Church. Even so, working to the libretto that (like *The Apostles*) he himself had constructed from the Bible, Elgar continued to compose the music for the oratorio during the first half of 1906. Work on it proceeded during a second visit to the United States (where he conducted both *The Apostles* and *The Dream of Gerontius*) and it was completed in August, in time for him to conduct the emotional and successful première in Birmingham in October. The trilogy, though, was to remain a headless torso, for a year later Elgar concluded that he could not complete it and, despite occasional attempts by friends and colleagues to revive his interest in the project, he was to write no more oratorios.

It was now orchestral music that dominated his output. In 1907 he returned to some of his childhood sketches, reworking them as the first of his *Wand of Youth* suites, but he had an altogether grander work in mind: his First Symphony. He began work on it in June 1907, and the diary maintained by Alice reflects something of his progress and of his fluctuating moods. The celebrated conductor Hans Richter, to whom the symphony was eventually dedicated, paid several visits to Hereford to discuss details, and Richter it was who conducted the Hallé Orchestra at the first performance in December 1908. London heard it four days later, again with Richter conducting a piece that he described as 'the greatest symphony of modern times', and the public seemed to concur.

For the first time, at the age of fifty-one, Sir Edward Elgar had achieved an unqualified success, but, predictably, amid the welter of praise he still found time to complain about the bills and to express his dissatisfaction with matters generally. Partly as a reaction to the intense activity of composing, perhaps, and when he could avoid conducting engagements, he retreated to an outhouse at 'Plâs Gwyn', where he indulged his enthusiasm for chemical experiments, but in the spring the Elgars went to Italy on holiday, returning via Bavaria. That seems to have rekindled the urge to compose, with a part-song, *Go, Song of Mine*, dedicated to Alice Stuart Wortley, the inspirational 'Windflower' of Elgar's imagination; the extensive correspondence between the two is testimony to her influence, and the deeply emotional

The composer's enthusiasm for scientific experiments led to him converting an outhouse into a makeshift laboratory at 'Plâs Gwyn'.

Violin Concerto, which he began to compose immediately upon his return from holiday, is said to contain her 'soul'.

The idea of a concerto had been with him for some time – probably since the redoubtable violinist Fritz Kreisler had asked him for one in 1906 – and, although it was another violinist, W. H. ('Billy') Reed, who offered practical support and advice during the work's composition, it was Kreisler to whom the honour of giving the first performance was granted. Elgar himself conducted the first performance in November 1910 and, like the symphony of two years earlier, it was an immediate success, confirming Elgar as the pre-eminent composer of the day. This was reinforced by the award of the Order of Merit in the Coronation honours list of 1911, recognition that Elgar did seem to appreciate, even to the extent of believing that its significance was insufficiently appreciated by the people of Worcestershire and asking Troyte Griffith to publicise its importance. Despite the honours, the public success and the reputation enjoyed by his music, it is clear that Elgar's basic insecurity remained.

Elgar in court dress, wearing the insignia of the Order of Merit.

He composed a March for the Coronation of George V, but his main creative energies during the early months of 1911 were spent on his Second Symphony. He himself said that

> The spirit of the whole work is intended to be high & pure joy: there are retrospective passages of sadness but the whole of the sorrow is smoothed out & ennobled in the last movement which ends in a calm … mood.

Elgar with his wife and daughter on the steps of 'Plâs Gwyn' in 1910; the photograph was taken by Percy Hull, assistant organist at Hereford Cathedral.

However, it is not certain that the audience at the first performance appreciated the often reflective nature of the music, and reaction was muted. Elgar himself was moved to exclaim to Billy Reed, who was leading the orchestra, 'What's the matter with them, Billy? They sit there like a lot of stuffed pigs'. The composer may have been disappointed, but the critics' reaction was not unfavourable, although it was to be some years before the true quality of the symphony was widely appreciated.

It was to be the last music of any significance that Elgar composed in Hereford, for on New Year's Day of 1912 the family moved into 'Severn House', a large house in Hampstead that Elgar described as 'very comfortable & so quiet'. Not only was this property well suited to his social standing but it was one that presented him with the opportunity to compose in comparative peace.

London and Sussex, 1912–20

It is probable that Alice had always considered London as the acme for Edward and of her ambitions for him. She had had to bear the scorn of her relatives and had surrendered her place in society; the Elgars had been forced to abandon London and return to the provinces at the beginning of Edward's career and, despite the public recognition accorded to her husband over the past decade and more, this grand house in London with the opportunity to entertain wealthy and influential people would have set the seal upon her satisfaction at Edward's success. For Elgar himself it was convenient. His journeys to London from Malvern and then Hereford had become increasingly frequent as his reputation grew; his publishers were in London, he had been appointed

The interior of 'Severn House' in Hampstead, showing the impressive music-room.

Alice Elgar in court dress, 1912.

permanent conductor to the London Symphony Orchestra, influential supporters and friends such as Frank Schuster and Sir Edward Speyer lived there, and it did provide the opportunity for the Elgars to socialise.

With friends and many of those involved professionally in the business of making music Elgar was amusing, boisterous and generous, and they saw a very different side from the sometimes prickly and irritable composer and conductor experienced by those with whom he felt ill at ease and whom he thought less than professional in their approach to music. He could be quick to take offence and he quarrelled with Stanford, for example, who had been among the first to recognise his genius and who had nominated him as a member of the Athenaeum Club as early as 1902, but he certainly responded to the loyalty, understanding and no little admiration that he was accorded by friends and many of his colleagues.

Above and opposite: 'Kindly do not smoke in the hall or staircase': a detail
of Elgar's joke fragment of an imaginary cantata for Sir Edward Speyer
and a large orchestra, setting the words of his host's injunction and liberally

In 1914 he was taken by the conductor Landon Ronald to the recording
studios of the Gramophone Company (later His Master's Voice) and
there met Fred Gaisberg, who as early as 1902 had had the perspicacity
to recognise the talent of Enrico Caruso, and who constantly prompted

embellished with billowing clouds of smoke, a typical example of the composer's sense of humour.

and encouraged Elgar to record his own music. With his abiding interest in scientific matters and recognising the enormous educational potential of the gramophone, the composer can have needed little encouragement, despite the primitive recording techniques of the period, and he became

Sir Edward Elgar in 1915: watercolour sketch by Percy Anderson painted at 'The Hut', Schuster's house at Bray, Berkshire, where Elgar was staying at the time.

The first recording by the composer was made in January 1914 at the Gramophone Company's premises at 21 City Road, London; the primitive recording techniques, with the orchestra, led by W. H. Reed, playing directly into a huge horn, are clearly demonstrated.

Elgar at his study in 'Severn House'.

the first major composer to commit to record his interpretation of his own works. He made his first record later in 1914, conducting a small orchestra in his own *Carissima*, a new piece that had received its first performance earlier in the year.

That Elgar was a consummate professional in his music-making cannot be gainsaid, but it remains difficult to reconcile the bluff, country-loving, pipe-smoking image that Elgar presented with the sophisticate capable of being absorbed into the London of the early twentieth century, and the truth is that Elgar himself never did abandon his personal preference for the shires. In later life he said:

> I am still at heart the dreamy child who used to be found in the reeds by Severn side with a sheet of paper trying to fix the sounds & longing for something very great.

There is, too, the extent to which he found London inimical to composition and the inspiration that, by contrast, he derived from the power and the peace of the countryside. It is little wonder that Elgar became more and more depressed, seeing little hope for the future, though a brief holiday did again spark the muse and Elgar resumed work on something he had considered some years earlier: a symphonic poem on the subject of *Falstaff*. It was performed at the Leeds Festival in 1913 but failed to please, and that, coming on top of the decision

Elgar (lower left) 'on parade' with the Hampstead Special Constabulary.

of the London Symphony Orchestra not to renew his contract as principal conductor, can only have added to the composer's deep pessimism.

Added to this, the international situation was causing concern, however much the pleasure-loving post-Edwardian London society may have wished to ignore it. On 4th August 1914 Germany, already at war with Russia and France, invaded neutral Belgium and Britain entered the war, with Elgar moved to write *Carillon*, an accompanied recitation setting patriotic words by the Belgian poet Emile Cammaerts. Its success with the sympathetic public was enormous, but if anyone thought that the Elgar of *Land of Hope and Glory* was about to produce a series of jingoistic pieces calculated to bolster public enthusiasm for the war against Germany they had greatly misunderstood their man.

True, he did volunteer for service and enrolled in the Hampstead Special Constabulary, later transferring to the Volunteer Reserve, but, already pessimistic about the future, he became increasingly disturbed by the progress of the war and the appalling slaughter that was taking place on the Western Front, where the Allies and German forces sacrificed hundreds of lives over feet of ground. His deep distress extended not so much to the men – mankind after all had brought this upon itself, however much individuals may be mere pawns – but to the animals used for hauling gun carriages and other vehicles. 'I walk round and round this room cursing God for allowing dumb brutes to be tortured – let Him kill his human beings but how CAN HE? Oh, my horses', he railed in a letter to his friend Frank Schuster.

1915 saw the production of *The Starlight Express* with incidental music by Elgar, a virtual retreat into the dreamland of childhood, but the realities of war continued to intrude. As late as 1918, for instance, Charles Mott, a baritone whom Elgar regarded highly and who had appeared in *The Starlight Express* and in his 1917 song cycle *The Fringes of the Fleet*, was killed in Flanders, but by then Elgar had already composed what probably reflected his most deeply felt emotions about the war: *The Spirit of England*. It comprises three songs for a soloist, chorus and orchestra, setting poems by Laurence Binyon, the third of which, *For the Fallen*, and Elgar's dedication of the work to 'the memory of our glorious men, with a special thought for the Worcesters' indicates the true character of the piece. There is nothing of vainglory and militarism, nothing of pomp and circumstance here.

Nor was there consolation to be found in the London musical scene, which Elgar himself described as 'moribund – the conductors dance over some exhumed corpses & the poorer the music the more acrobatic are the (mis)interpreters'. From the outset composition in London had proved difficult and, appreciating this, Alice sought an oasis where her beloved husband could find the peace he needed. She discovered this in 'Brinkwells', a small cottage in the heart of Sussex, and the

'Brinkwells' in Sussex, where Elgar composed his series of great chamber works.

'If ever after I'm dead you hear someone whistling this tune on the Malvern Hills, don't be alarmed, it's only me': Elgar on a theme from his 'Cello Concerto.

Elgar with the 'cellist Beatrice Harrison, who was the soloist in the first recording of the 'Cello Concerto at the end of 1919.

Elgars moved there in 1917 while retaining their London house.

The peace and tranquillity of 'Brinkwells' had the desired effect. Elgar's health, always uncertain when he was in London, improved following a minor operation to remove a septic tonsil, and he embarked upon a burst of creative energy that resulted in one of his acknowledged masterpieces, the 'Cello Concerto, with its haunting suggestion of a world lost, and three towering works of the chamber music repertoire: a violin sonata, a piano quintet and a string quartet. All of them contain passages of great lyricism, but equally all are imbued with touches of either the macabre or an innate pessimism, and it is difficult not to believe that they are coloured by the war and the effect it had had upon the composer. The Quartet and the Quintet received their first public performance at the Wigmore Hall, London, in May 1919, when they were performed by Elgar's friend Billy Reed and some of his colleagues, and the two works were quickly absorbed into the repertoire. Elgar, however, never returned to either form and indeed he now had pressing personal concerns. The Elgars had decided that they needed

Programme of the first performance of the String Quartet and the Piano Quintet, both featuring Reed's quartet.

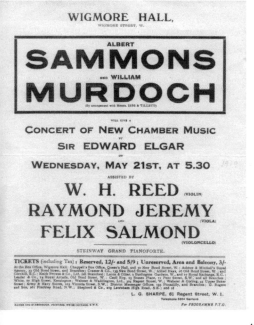

The violinist Billy Reed, who offered Elgar both friendship and technical advice.

to sell 'Severn House' and Alice, who had reached the age of seventy, was troubled with a recurrent cold; during 1920 her health gave cause for increasing concern, and she died on 7th April.

Edward was distraught. His letters to friends are an outpouring of grief and reveal the depth of his feelings at the loss of the one person who had supported, encouraged and sustained him through three decades, and without whom, one may safely say, he would not have become the important figure that he did. Elgar himself admitted to a colleague that all he had done was owing to her, and his sense of loss was laid bare in a moving letter to Ernest Newman in which he wrote:

> I tried to break the emptiness of the change by allowing the Quartet [i.e. Reed's]
> to rehearse here, but – without the hostess: my God.

That void permeated his ability and his will to compose – as subsequent events were to show.

The final years, 1921–34

Lady Alice Elgar was buried at St Wulstan's Church in Malvern Wells, with Reed and his colleagues playing the slow movement from the String Quartet at the ceremony. Elgar did not, as one might imagine, immediately abandon London for Worcestershire, but he did retreat to 'Brinkwells' for much of the first year. Slowly he began to pick up

This delicate watercolour of Sir Edward Elgar was painted by Percy Anderson soon after the death of Lady Elgar.

Study of Carice Elgar painted shortly before her wedding in 1922 and apparently a companion piece to the watercolour of her father (page 49).

the threads of his life but, although he did attend concerts of his music and even conducted some of them, composition played little part in it, with little more than some transcriptions of Bach completed during the first two years. 'Severn House' was sold in 1921 but Elgar was unable to buy 'Brinkwells' as he would have liked, and he took a flat in St James's Place in the West End of London, near to London's theatreland and convenient for Brook's, the elite club that he had joined and which, with its strong historical tradition, he greatly enjoyed.

There is no doubt that, despite a number of abiding friendships, Elgar was now a very lonely man, and out of sympathy with the times, both social and musical – and though he did help a number of younger composers, notably Arthur Bliss and Arnold Bax, his relationship with

Elgar with his three dogs in 1923 at 'Napleton Grange', Kempsey, in Worcestershire, one of the rented properties he occupied after his wife's death.

them was always unpredictable. His isolation was increased in 1922 by the marriage of his only daughter Carice to Samuel Blake, although they did remain in close contact. He sought companionship from his dogs, something not possible while his wife was alive as she disliked animals, and he spent some time in Worcestershire, visiting his sister in Bromsgrove. He toyed with the idea of returning to Malvern and even went so far as to ask Troyte to find him somewhere suitable, not too far from St Wulstan's Church, where Alice was buried. Nothing came of it, however, and Elgar divided his time between his flat in London and a rented house in Kempsey on the eastern side of the Severn.

During these arid years Elgar, in the depths of his despair and loneliness, confided to Alice Stuart Wortley that 'my barren honours are dust' and professed to have little or no interest in music. The musical world continued to have an interest in Elgar, however, and gradually he was drawn back into it. He was prevailed upon to compose music for the British Empire Exhibition at Wembley in 1924, and in the following month he was appointed to the vacant post of Master of

Elgar conducting at the British Empire Exhibition, 1924.

Elgar in 1929 with one of
the gramophones presented
to him by HMV.

the King's Musick, a position within the establishment that he had
argued should be retained because of its historic and symbolic
significance. It certainly reflected his standing in the country, but it
did not spur him to resume serious composing and such works as did
issue from his pen were generally slight, while his general attitude
and comments suggested that he would far rather be at his club or
watching horse-racing than at his desk working. Now in his sixties,
he still presented a distinguished appearance, 5 feet 10 inches (1.78
metres) tall with a prominent aquiline nose, a large moustache and
hair already grey turning white. Superficially at least, he retained the
air of the retired military man, or possibly a country gentleman – an
image that he seems to have cultivated, being not free of a measure of
pomposity – and he was liable to attend the annual Three Choirs Festival
in his court dress of velvet coat and breeches, thus reinforcing the
contemporary view of him as a figure from the past.

Meanwhile the recording industry had been developing electric
reproduction of music, a significant advance on the pre-electric recordings

The elderly Elgar and the young Yehudi Menuhin at the time of the recording of the Violin Concerto.

which Elgar had been amongst the earliest of British composers to pioneer. Fred Gaisberg of His Master's Voice (HMV) was quick to draw the composer's attention to the advantages of the new system, and from 1926 until shortly before his death Elgar was closely involved with HMV in preserving for posterity his interpretation of many of his own creations. These included the 'Cello Concerto (with Beatrice Harrison as the soloist) and the Violin Concerto; the latter, recorded as late as 1932, has become one of the most celebrated of those recordings because of the collaboration between the seventy-five year old composer and the fifteen year old prodigy Yehudi Menuhin, with Elgar's enthusiastic endorsement of the youngster's playing followed by his expressed wish to leave the recording session as soon as possible in order to go to Newmarket races.

By then there had been further honours: the KCVO (Knight Commander of the Royal Victorian Order) in 1928, and a baronetcy in 1931; it was a far cry from his humble beginnings but the emotional pull of those early years remained strong and as his title he chose 'Broadheath'. There was one further honour, the GCVO (Knight Grand Cross of the Royal Victorian Order), which was awarded in 1933, but by then Elgar was terminally ill. Despite the public esteem in which the composer was held, however, his music was no longer as popular and, moreover, his ability was again coming under attack – on this occasion from Edward Dent, Professor of Music at Cambridge, who, conveniently ignoring the praise he had heaped upon Elgar's chamber works, criticised his music as vulgar and compared the composer unfavourably with Stanford and Parry. Elgar's supporters rallied to him, but the resulting controversy can only have been unwelcome and even hurtful to the still basically insecure Elgar and must have confirmed in him his youthful prejudice against the academic establishment.

His choral music had become a staple part of the Three Choirs Festival, held in the cathedral cities of Worcester, Hereford and Gloucester in turn, and the elderly composer was a regular visitor to the Festival. He remained keenly aware of contemporary events and drew Troyte Griffith's attention to the creation by Barry Jackson of the Malvern Festival, arguing that they needed to 'be there'. Elgar certainly was, for even at the opening Festival in 1929, which contained no music and featured George Bernard Shaw's *The Apple Cart*, he opened the exhibition devoted to Shaw, and the occasion saw an exchange of compliments and expressions of friendship between the two men. Shaw had been an admirer of Elgar's music for some years, even going so far in 1920 as to write publicly that he thought it bore 'the stigmata of

Elgar in court dress at the Hereford Three Choirs Festival, 1933, with Percy Hull, the Hereford Cathedral organist.

immortality', and the two played duets together at a private function during the Festival.

Elgar had moved back to Worcester in 1929, to 'Marl Bank', a large house in the city, and this was to be his home for the remaining five years of his life. His daughter Carice was a frequent visitor, and Elgar found some consolation in his two remaining dogs, his 'beloved companions'. Two years later he renewed his friendship with Ernest Newman, writing that his 'interest in our art is now very slight or perhaps, I shd say, dead', and excusing himself for not having written on the grounds that he had thought their friendship was mainly because of what he was pleased to call 'my former activity'. He established a friendly relationship with Vaughan Williams, while old friends such as Billy Reed and Troyte Griffith remained in close contact with him.

There is some evidence during those final years of a reawakening of interest in composing, with the incidental music to a play entitled *Beau Brummel* written in 1928, his only work for brass band, *Severn Suite*, in 1930, and the *Nursery Suite* (using some themes from his youth) in 1931, but, as on other occasions in the past, it seems to have taken a young violinist, in this case Vera Hockman, to provide real

Above: Elgar and his daughter Carice in the garden of 'Marl Bank'.

Elgar with Marco and Mina, *c.*1933.

inspiration for the elderly composer. Thus, the last two years of his life are peppered with thoughts of major projects to be completed: an opera based on a play by Ben Jonson, a piano concerto that Elgar had worked on intermittently over many years, and, most controversially, a projected third symphony for which the composer, prompted by Bernard Shaw, had obtained a commission from the BBC. Elgar would complete none of them.

In October 1933 he was taken to a Worcester nursing home for an operation but was found to have terminal cancer. He suffered acute pain during the next few months and, despite continuing to affirm that he no longer had any faith in an after-life or the teachings of the Church, he was actually given the last rites in November. He survived, however, and was strong enough to return home to 'Marl Bank' in January, where many of his friends and colleagues came to see him – Griffith, Newman, Gaisberg who brought him the latest recordings of his music and who arranged a live link-up with the recording studio in London, and Billy Reed, to whom Elgar entrusted the sketches of

During the final months of his life the composer was visited by many friends, including Fred Gaisberg of HMV, seen here with Carice Elgar Blake.

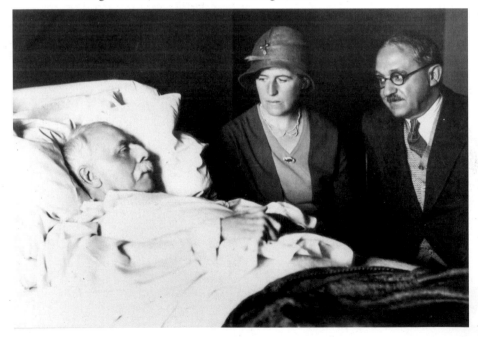

Above: 'I am still at heart the dreamy boy … by the reeds by Severn side' — the confluence of the rivers Severn and Teme, where Elgar expressed the wish that his ashes be scattered.

his unfinished Third Symphony with the suggestion that they should be burned as no one would understand them. In the event Reed did no such thing, and it is a matter of history that in 1997 Anthony Payne completed his realisation of the Symphony.

The composer died on 23rd February 1934. He had earlier expressed the wish that his ashes be scattered at the confluence of the rivers Teme and Severn, but just before his death he was seen

Elgar's grave in St Wulstan's churchyard, Malvern Wells.

by a Jesuit father who stated that Elgar had reaffirmed his Catholic faith, and in acknowledgement of that the composer was buried with his wife at St Wulstan's Church in Malvern Wells. It is a modest resting place, perhaps surprisingly so for a man who had achieved such fame, but not inappropriate to one of humble origins who had moreover retained a love of his native Worcestershire. In any event, it may be of little moment where a man rests since the greatness of one who transcended all handicaps to become a household name and a symbol of national pride continues where it matters most – in his music.

The cottage and garden at Broadheath, little changed in its outward appearance but now converted to a museum dedicated to the life and work of Sir Edward Elgar.

Finding out more about Sir Edward Elgar

The most comprehensive collection of material by and about Sir Edward Elgar is to be found at the **Elgar Birthplace**, Crown East Lane, Lower Broadheath, Worcestershire WR2 6RH, just 3 miles (5 km) west of Worcester (telephone: 01905 333224; website: www.elgarmuseum.org; email: birthplace@elgarmuseum.org). The Birthplace cottage and the adjacent visitor centre are open to the public, and the displays include original manuscripts and letters, portraits and photographs, programmes and personal artefacts, and there is the opportunity of hearing a wide range of music by the composer. In addition there is an extensive archive with on-site research facilities; prior booking is essential for those wishing to use the research collections.

Other major collections of Elgar material are held at the **British Library** in London (website: www.bl.uk) and the **University of Birmingham** (website: www.special-coll.bham.ac.uk; email: special-collections@bham.ac.uk), where Elgar was Peyton Professor of Music from 1902 to 1905, and a number of individual manuscripts are held by major British universities and music colleges.

The **Elgar Society**, with its strong international links, is active in promoting interest in Elgar and his music, and publishes a journal and a separate newsletter three times a year; details of membership benefits and subscription rates are available from the Elgar Birthplace at the above address or from the Honorary Membership Secretary, David Morris, 2 Marriott's Close, Haddenham, Buckinghamshire HP17 8BT (website: www.elgar.org; email: membership@elgar.org).

Further reading

There have been numerous biographies and studies of Elgar since the appearance of the first of them (by Robert J. Buckley) as early as 1905, but the most comprehensive are R. Anderson's *Elgar* (Dent, 1993), M. Kennedy's *Portrait of Elgar* (Oxford University Press, third edition, 1987) and J. Northrop Moore's *Edward Elgar: A Creative Life* (Oxford University Press, 1984).

Michael Kennedy's subsequent book *The Life of Elgar* (Cambridge University Press, 2004) incorporates research carried out since the publication of his earlier *Portrait of Elgar* but does not entirely supersede it, while Jerrold Northrop Moore is responsible for a number of other major works detailing Elgar's relationships with his publishers, friends and colleagues as demonstrated through the composer's extensive correspondence.

Among earlier biographies mention should be made of Percy Young's *Elgar, O.M.* (Collins, second edition, 1973), while reminiscences by others who knew Elgar include W. H. Reed's *Elgar As I Knew Him* (Gollancz, third impression, 1978; first published 1936), Mrs R. C. Powell's *Edward Elgar: Memories of a Variation* (Methuen, revised third edition, 1994), Rosa Burley and F. Carruthers's *Edward Elgar: the Record of a Friendship* (Barrie & Jenkins, 1972) and E. Wulstan Atkins's *The Elgar–Atkins Friendship* (David & Charles, 1984).

The monographs and articles dealing with individual works and detailed aspects or periods of Elgar's life are legion and readers wishing to explore those published before 1993 could with advantage consult Geoffrey Hoskins's comprehensive bibliography, printed in *The Music Review*, 54, 1, but also issued as a separate offprint. A number of important monographs have been published by Elgar Editions; a full list of available titles can be found on the Elgar Society's website (www.elgar.org) and are available either from the society or through the Elgar Birthplace (www.elgarmuseum.org/trolleyed). Extensive research into Elgar's life and music continues, and a significant proportion of this is published in the journal of the Elgar Society.

Principal events

1857   Born 2nd June at Broadheath.
1859   Family moved back to Worcester.
1863   Moved to 10 High Street, Worcester (the Elgar Brothers' shop).
1878   Played in the Three Choirs Festival Orchestra for the first time.
1885   Succeeded his father as organist of St George's Church, Worcester.
1888   Composed *Salut d'amour*.
1889   Married Caroline Alice Roberts; moved to London.
1890   Daughter Carice born; *Froissart* performed at Worcester Three Choirs.
1891   Returned to Worcestershire and settled in Malvern.
1898   Composed *Caractacus*.
1899   Composed *Enigma Variations*.
1900   Composed *The Dream of Gerontius*; awarded doctorate by Cambridge University.
1901   Composed first *Pomp and Circumstance Marches*.
1903   Composed *The Apostles*.
1904   Knighted; moved to Hereford.
1905   Gave first lecture as Peyton Professor of Music, University of Birmingham.
1906   Composed *The Kingdom*.
1908   Composed First Symphony.
1910   Composed Violin Concerto.
1911   Awarded Order of Merit; completed Second Symphony.
1912   Moved to London.
1914   Conducted first gramophone recording (*Carissima*).
1917   Rented 'Brinkwells' in Sussex.
1918   Composed Violin Sonata and String Quartet.
1919   Composed Piano Quintet and 'Cello Concerto.
1920   Wife died on 7th April in London.
1924   Appointed Master of the King's Musick.
1928   Awarded KCVO.
1929   Purchased 'Marl Bank' in Worcester, his last home.
1931   Made Baronet (of Broadheath).
1932   Conducted recording of Violin Concerto with Menuhin as soloist.
1933   Awarded GCVO.
1934   Died 23rd February at home in Worcester.

Index

Page numbers in italic refer to illustrations